Portia White

A PORTRAIT IN WORDS

Poetry by GEORGE ELLIOTT CLARKE

Art by LARA MARTINA

NIMBUS
PUBLISHING
— NIMBUS.CA —

Nimbus Publishing Limited
3660 Strawberry Hill Street, Halifax, NS, B3K 5A9
(902) 455-4286 nimbus.ca

Printed and bound in Canada
NB1284

Cover design: Heather Bryan
Interior design: Peggy Issenmen, Peggy + Co Design
Editor: Paul Zemokhol
Editor for the press: Whitney Moran
Proofreaders: Sylvia Hamilton & Elizabeth Eve

Photos of Portia White and family provided by the author.

Library and Archives Canada Cataloguing in Publication

Title: Portia White : a portrait in words / poetry by George Elliott Clarke ;
art by Lara Martina.
Names: Clarke, George Elliott, author. | Martina, Lara, 1955- illustrator.
Description: A poem.
Identifiers: Canadiana (print) 20190156147 | Canadiana (ebook) 20190156597 |
ISBN 9781771086974
(hardcover) | ISBN 9781771086981 (HTML)
Subjects: LCSH: White, Portia, 1911-1968—Poetry.
Classification: LCC PS8555.L3748 P67 2019 | DDC C811/.54—dc23

Nimbus Publishing acknowledges the financial support for its publishing activities
from the Government of Canada, the Canada Council for the Arts, and from the
Province of Nova Scotia. We are pleased to work in partnership with the Province
of Nova Scotia to develop and promote our creative industries for the benefit of all
Nova Scotians.

Contents

De la fealdad del hombre a la belleza
Del Universo asciendo....
—José Martí, "Marzo"

For Geraldine Elizabeth Clarke (1939–2000)
& William Lloyd Clarke (1935–2005):
Adepts, Believers, African Baptists.

Preface

*A*lthough *Art* is *vero*, never
Falso, my *Portia* is ever
A portrait, only *partially*
An autobiographically
Accurate depiction. I take
Liberties—poetic—and take
License to version her story
In her voice, to tell *History*
Who she was—as I hear her say
Or sing. I confirm facts, but say
Also what I think she'd've* said.
(That's one benefit of the dead—
To voice now from beyond the grave
Apt opinions we let em have….)
One other cool truth about the dead?
They're out of *Time*! Timeless, instead,
Their autobios range, careless
About *Chronology*. Fearless,
They die, give birth, learn to talk, shape
Trousseaus, get born, let *Time* escape
All bounds, all order, every tense!
The consequence of each sequence?
Equivalent *Ambivalence*:
So "now" and "then" shift precedence.

Thus, World War Two ends and the First
One begins. Why not? Each accursed
Conflict's equally horrendous:
Neither one a crescendo was!
From the perspective of the dead,
Neither "first" nor "last" ends ahead,

---

* "She would have": Contracted to—and pronounced as—two syllables.

Since all die, since *Time*'s as endless
As *Death*. So, Portia may witness
Early on what should happen late,
For, dead, she lives in timeless state.)

Strict readers, perhaps, may prefer
Cold marble's dictator-rigour
(Ideal for dour graveyards), rather
Than prisms of chromatic flux
Where *Perception*'s collage deluxe,
Not inflexible, where thoughts change
And intersect as thoughts arrange.
I prefer living colours, not dead,
Zombie-sombre shades, dull as lead.
So, my *Portia White* (but perhaps
Not yours) lauded Fascist collapse,
May have boogied with Ellington
(Or wished to), liked *Elegance*, on
Stage and off, and may have dispatched
Haligonians to pinch latched
Hooch in the V.E. Day *Riot*—
That *louche*, Halifax *Disquiet*.
Honest are these tales? I don't know:
They are hearsay, but seem to show
As down-to-earth the idolized
Miss White, not so "italicized,"
Nor haughty, but spectacular
With earthy *Mirth*; vernacular
Even, sometimes in talk (even
Though she spoke Queen's English, seven
Times out of ten). Yep, my diction
For *Portia* swears by pulp fiction!
(Like some throwback historian—
Or bard—Tory, Victorian—

I use old-fashioned contractions,
Like *o'er*, to sound syllables *once*
That could be sounded more. Also
I use slang—po-mo* gone retro.
And oft I skip apostrophes—
So "them" is "em" and "ing"—for ease—
Is "in." Whyn't** let airborne commas
Boomerang to The Bahamas?!!)

But who can say for sure what words
Portia'd choose if she'd fresh speak words?
We leaf through sheets—*recto, verso*—
Of letters, as mute as Braille, so
Silent—like dead scripts we can't know.
So, yep, my bio's a dumb-show—
Especially if you do not
Voice these inklings that shadow *Thought*!
Then again, inescapable
Is my *Portia* as part-fable
(Maybe fiction), despite checked facts
I've accessed—wielding pen-as-axe***
And ink-as-sax. Something there is
About *Poetry* that insists
On *Imagination* as rule
That overrules scholar or school.
Nevertheless, please rest assured
That my *Portia White* ain't obscured
By my predilections for word
And plot. I've not caricatured
Her character? I dare say so:
But only my portrait's on show—
And on trial, which must be the case.
But still you will come face-to-face
With *a* "Portia," whose life outshines
All brilliance this black ink divines....

* Postmodern.
** "Why not" is contracted to one syllable.
*** Do read it *doubly* as the slang term for *guitar*.

1 – Command Performance
for Elizabeth II (1964)

"*Music* is perfume"—I do think—
If notes are flowers, if scents are ink;
And songs are bouquets that arise
From vases of throats, and surprise
The air with *Beauty*, so one's stunned—
Astonished, by florals summoned
On scales limber as trellises
(Such sweet solace for palaces)—
Petals of lilts and leaves of trills—
Aromas only stifling stills.

I do think so, as my voice flutes
Vines of song no critic uproots,
For I'm myself a crown jewel, fit
For The Queen, her Royal Visit
To Charlottetown, Prince Edward Isle
(Where Green Gables' green goes viral),
To ope the Confederation
Centre, where conceived the nation
Nearly a century before—
Did top-hat gents, posed, portraying *Power*....

But here's The Queen in spanking white,
A gleaming gown, all spiffy, quite,
And the halo-like crown she sports,
Is laurels, bright, where light cavorts,
Courting diamonds and portly gems.

Flourishing serenading hymns—
Slaves' spirituals I warble as
A vocal artiste (no mere *Jazz*
Singer), a contralto, in mink
And pearls, spot-lit. What should I think,
Opening the treasure chest that's
My heart and lungs; to recall what's
Sorrow, those coffle-raised tunes (gold
To my silver tongue)? Why withhold
What *noblesse oblige* obliges?
To dust off *History*'s digests
And chorus Potentates with *Truth*
(It's what I do—have done—since youth);
I shan't schmooze; soothe with serenades!
I see slaves shackled in parades
When The Queen's ancestors—enthroned—
Numbered my ancestors as "owned"—
As "Africans" judged good as cash;
Who toiled neath smack and crack of lash.

Now here I stand, august, fab, suave—
Granddaughter of a Dixie slave—
And daughter of a father grand
(The first Black to Brit troops command).
That's I, Portia, Reverend Captain
Dr. William Andrew White's kin—
His girl, Nova Scotia's trophy—
Strong songstress, strophe to strophe—
In Truro's Zion church choir or
On stage, rhyming *Moor* and *Amour*.

Or was I souvenir also
Of *Slavery*, of chains, of *Woe*—
Despite being born free in the North,
To parents, conscious of our worth?

Still, I feel conviction to live
As black folks' Representative—
As unconquered *Genius*, with sass—
A chatelaine's chic gravitas—
And blister ears with *Trouble*'s songs—
Spiritual salvos out my lungs—
To be a diva, or maestro,
Of *Labour*, sweat for each "Bravo!";
To bruit *History*'s gospel, I
Wail, bawl, hiss, caterwaul, and sigh
Words as fluid as currency.

(The *Revolution*? An LP—
A vinyl disc—usually black,
Spinning with a stylus in track
At 33 gyres per minute—
Making every home a senate,
A parliament, a court, of *Song*.)

And so, I'm right where I belong
Couriering emotions (what
Singing does best, besting poet
And painter), to unfurl my voice—
Exposing stabbed-heart pangs. That choice—
To build a pyramid of notes,
Ladder it, descanting (no doubts
Endowed), and steadily to rise—
Thanks to the passport that's each prize
Or anti-gravity applause,
The critic's praise that cancels laws,
So music notes foster bank notes
Or gold medals—and judges' votes
That award silver cups, then calls
To perform at Manhattan balls—
Or curtsy—for Queen Liz.
                              (Why not?
To *Wealth* and *Fame* was she begot.

But I expend my voice to retire
My debts—my deficits—of dire,
Salt-spray *Apartheid*, Maritime
Black-and-white *Segregation*, rime
On walls and blight on crops, the ill,
The sick, the rhyme between Beechville
(One of dozens of black locales
That are Ol' Scotia's "Negro cells")
And Bantustan (South Africa's
Townships—or jails—anathemas
For Native Blacks). My confession:
I sing of the Great Depression—
When capitalists proved cannibals;
But I use muted decibels.
I'm not Paul Robeson radical
("Black and Red") nor a hoofin gal
Like Josey Baker (who's in France—
Hellion, warbling *Recalcitrance*—
To retaliate—with *Talent*—
Versus Yahoos.) Oh, to lament
That audience of mannequins—
White-hood Klan, pith-helmet Britons,
Whacking the "Coloured" colonies
(As do the French who scandalize—
Axing heads off kids in Vietnam
And North Africa). Yes, I am
Not Marian Anderson—that
U.S. *chanteuse*—poised, hailed—who scat
Sang Constitution rights, to tout
Freedom, *Equality*, to flout
Lynch mobs—sired by *Segregation*,
Whose mastery is *Castration*—
Those hysterical varmints who
Creep from pond-scum or slime or zoo,
To storm and sting, poisonous as
Swastika-shaped tarantulas.

The "Hateful States" ain't my nation!
(Contained's their *Contamination*?
But uncontained's my elation!)

Ah, *Success* is *Circulation*!
To vault one's voice from vinyl discs—
To sculpt a masterpiece (sound risks)
Out of rags—odds and ends—of scores,
Blues and ballads; to compose roars—
Tunes, sour and sweet, songs seditious—
The spirituals, tunes "malicious"
To slavers and pharaohs because,
Sooner or later, *Song* outlives us:
It's not only ornamental
To *Silence*, but elemental—
Outlasting each and every reign:
Monarchs perish, but songs remain.

I needn't shuffle in *Ragtime*
Spoofs, nor bustle in pantomime
Like a minstrel. But *Art's* status
Is never static. My practice?
To combine cantabile and
Folk lays, arias (on demand),
Plus Broadway hits and movie themes—
A repertoire of cadenced dreams—
To love—not dismantle—"Negro
Song," its genius—hymn'd *bel canto*—
Wherein voice is surf, insurgent—
My heart ardent, my pulse, urgent....

Her Majesty stops before me!
She states, "You rouse each artery;
Articulate all your marrow.
But there's no bile, only *Sorrow*,
Yet spectacularly spectral:
The *Blues* gone blue-blood, ventrical.
You neither relish nor garnish—
Miss White—nor polish nor varnish

History's woes, the *Time*'s distress!
Victoria Spivey's likeness
(Just as queen-like)—not Jezebel's
Or Aunt Jemima's—thy dazzle's
Implacable, not cosmetic.
It adds up—like arithmetic.
As upright and pure as the sun—
Outdo Callas (her airs outdone).
You surmount the stage to surplus
Superlatives, glow—glamorous,
Bow for bouquets, in *Lucence* bathe;
So critics, speechless, lose all faith
In synonyms. You bamboozle
Reviewers, kit and caboodle!
Empress, you so riffle the scores,
Pianists' fingers throb with sores,
And trumpets, narrow, hardly can
Squeeze out notes. (They squeak, squeal, scrape span-
And-spic the air!) Instrumental
(Who stage whispers a spiritual?)—
An erudite Aphrodite
(Unapologetic *Piety*)—
Uncompromising, luminous,
A humanist (thus humorous),
Thou knowest that *Philosophy*
Is the fount of *Music!*" Curtsy
Now, did she, The Queen, to me? Well,
I curtsied too: I'm no rebel,
Razzing The Crown. Yeah, I oppose
Quislings who betray—I mean, those
Who dispute *Democracy*—just
As I diss the tone-deaf! (Distrust
Those who'd slash violin strings, or
Saw through pianos, or injure
The bass, bashing—to smithereens—
A chest of harmonies!) The Queen's
Retinue now passes. My time
In the spotlight ebbs fast. I rhyme

What counts—to come to this high sum:

(*Praise*? That's wind!) What I have become
Is light, what's always news: Blameless
Starlight! To be never nameless,
Though an "off-colour white," being black—
With a sun-drenched being, bronze in plaque—
A halo'd sibyl neath an apse—
Light unlapsing though *Time* collapse.

"*I*, Portia May White, born on June
24, 1911:
1 of 13, but Shakespearean—
Dubbed for Will's lawyer-heroine—
And lagoon-gondola'd Venus—
That *Merchant of Venice* Princess....
The third child of Izie Dora
And William Andrew White, *fora**
Would open for me, so many,
I'd reap coins—the plural'd penny;
Let conductors posture or pose—
Batons that argue cons and pros
(Of *Music* versus rests, *Silence*
Versus *Clamour*), the wild vi'lins
Of lilting halls, tilting stages—
Sopranos vamping outrageous—
While contraltos conquer tenors....

A singer's at home with dancers—
Or actors or musicians at
Curtain, where goes round a doffed hat
For change, while clapping crowds apply—
Echo of each expensive cry
Purchased by ticket (paid *Attention*—
No deficit). May I mention?
Applause rings cheap, but very rich
That noise is, rushing the ears, which
Is lush reward for brash, flash words
Brandished, bandied, like clashing swords.
It was Helena Blackadar
Selected—prophetic—my star
Christening. I knew I'd perform
Under lights—hot and cold and warm—

* Plural of *forum*.

Yet suffer the loneliness of
Bus stations, train stations, for *Love*
Segues to *Loss* when one's solo,
Granting encores because YOLO,
Or navigating airports, ports,
And harbours far, so one weeps quartz—
Tears as hard as the heart is hard,
So one can smile where one is starred.

But Missionary Blackadar
Behaved as Christ-like avatar,
When she convinced Pops to leave
Virginia, where forebears did grieve
To slave, and grieved, and were bereaved,
And bereft. Helena conceived
The Nova Scotia location
For Papa's scolding vocation.
Thus, he came calling, then came I
Into North Star geography.
Both dad and daughter felt driven—
Like nails!—to clamp unto Heaven
Should God permit, but first live well,
Insisting, as Christians, to dwell
In *Harmony* and represent—
Like saints—a goodly government
Of dreams wondered, then won, then shared—
Escaping hells of souls ensnared—
That's what slaves wanted while enslaved:
To void or deprive the depraved
Of forced *Labour*. To toil for self
And roof, to stuff pots, not glean pelf....

So my sire desired to study
Theology; note sad, cruddy
Deeds sinners sin—despite stated,
Religious creeds. Dedicated
To song, though, was I, his daughter,
Who left in the choir a crater

Whenever I was absent. I
Was proud! I linked letters sprawled spry:
Cos-mo-pol-i-tan was the big
One. (Did that foresee that I'd gig
About the globe?) To me, back then,
Radio marked *Revolution*,
And nothing seemed more natural
Than sparking into song. So real
Seemed my girlhood lark: That I'd prance
And parade stages, and entrance
Eyes—and romance ears. Then, aged 8,
A music concert set me straight:
I'd live to sing! I'd thrive through *Song*!

Lucia di Lammermoor, among
Other operas, let me impart
Crescendos I crested by heart,
Which Papa loved because he cursed
Blues: He deemed doom-gloom tunes the worst—
"A lot of wailing by numbskulls—
The exhaustion of tuneless howls—
As if wolves had infiltrated
Ghettoes!" Right infuriated
Was he! "Copyrighted madness—
That's such pap! Abusing *Sadness*,
To mint lucre! Any airplay
Of those whining notes must dismay
All ears but the Devil's! Harrumph!
It's nasty—like Hitler's *Mein Kampf*!"

I had to exhale hymns, Gospel,
Songs operatic, classical,
While all us kids cleft wood, slung meals,
Soaped clothes, soaked dishes, fried up eels
(That leapt about the frying pan);
Baked bread, pies, muffins topped with bran;
Silver'd the table, all while *Song*
Planed from piano or each lung.

In school, I feared I was off-key:
Classmates hurled cutthroat looks at me
Whenever I sang. But, in truth,
My singing—though I was a youth—
Kayo'd my peers. Still, I felt some
Discontent, despite my freedom
And my friends. I think I was tense—
Nervous—because I had the sense
To know that I had to express
My soul. This talent I possess—
To shake the air with song—is vain
If I dare not deign to disdain
Disquiet, what diseases *Peace*,
For *Disturbance* must never cease
Whistling—bristling—thrown from the throat,
A crisp bellowing, nixing *Doubt*.

Studious, lusting for each book,
Lazed I, story-dazed, in each nook,
Pages outspread before my eyes—
Verses, encyclopedias,
Comics, romances, mysteries,
Heroes' bios, and histories:
Entire worlds could disappear, shift,
If my head turned, or pages drift.
Once my right reverend father
Caught me reading lines he'd rather
I didn't! Quick the "bad" book flew
Into purging flames, and I knew
Dad—fuming—was. But words once read,
Then remembered, are never dead,
And what's most sinful is not what's
Studied, but what's done. Jokes, pranks, plots,
Were too much fun to miss out on....

Such as, once when a neighbour man
Stepped below our window, and I
Dumped a pail of soapsuds—some lye
And foam—on his hat-bare, balding
Head. Dripping, but his look scalding,
The man bammed on our door. I cracked
It a peep, heard his complaint, backed
His outrage with my own grave face,
And pledged to put "rascals" in place,
Archly, I swore they'd be punished.
Huffing, he left. I, astonished
At how brazen my acting was—
Laughed like clowns in slapstick dramas—
Charlie Chaplin, Buster Keaton....
And when I saw rude words written
On a fence by sister Nettie,
I blackmailed missy real pretty!
Secret I'd keep her graffiti,
But eat her desserts. No pity
For Nettie: *Just* her just desserts!

In Bloomfield High School, we'd twirl skirts
Flirty with our knees. How daring
That was! But what was most cheering?
Carolling French, English, Spanish,
Italian, and German. My wish
Was to dish these tongues as delights
Sung; to spy PORTIA lit by lights—
Just as the yearbook predicted.

To *Fame* then was I addicted—
Even as a Bloomfield "flapper":
To star in every newspaper—
To shimmer in black ink neath red
Headlines, or be pictured instead—
Silvery. Could I wax golden?
Own gold records? *Fate* beholden?

III – From One War and Into the Second
(1915–1939)

*W*ar's ugly! But handsome are troops,
Our Canucks! Twice, ranked in armed groups,
In my childhood and youth, went they—
To save Britain from Germany
(Or, yes, to "save *Democracy*"?
But that's always what glib liars say!)

I was 3 when The Great War came—
And Reverend White added the name
"Captain," and boated off to France
To muddy boots in striking stance,
Heading up the "Black Battalion,"
The fine, No. 2 Construction
Brigade, who acted lumberjacks
Or carpenters, swinging down axe
Or hammer, by the Alps, distant
From the Western—and Eastern—Front,
Mobilized to lay railway ties,
They fought—with *Dismay* and *Surprise*—
Br'er Canucks—White Supremacists,
Who back-bit Captain White's blackness.

On one occasion, when the white
Soldiers, deranged, ganged up to fight
The black, Cap Pops slalomed his horse
Into the division, to force
Both sides—sliding wildly—to part—
Consolidate the common heart—
The union of the Dominion,
Canada, and the communion
Of Canadians that they were—
Also Christian, each officer
And soldier, black and white, they should
Equate each one equal. His good
Heroics saw no bloke loose blood,
Or act coward, or flounder in mud.

But though the battalion was far
From both fronts, victims of the war
Were swains and proles who swooned before
Mosquitoes malarial, or
Tuberculosis. Still, father
Scribed *billets-doux* daily. Rather
Would Mama have had her husband
Than mere letters. I understand:
But their love was never blighted,
And, once *Peace* bloomed, reunited
(Our boys demobilized), Captain
White (loving Jesus, not Joplin),
Regaled Mama for what seemed hours,
Describing putrescent sunflowers,
Ranged black cannons' "pitchforks of fire,"
The sun done drubbed in mud, the mire,
Vermin, and plagues! He took refuge
In The Bible, under deluge
Of miasma; leafed that novel
Of martyrs, as rain splashed hovel
And barracks. He heard of Ypres*—
Shells fanged—like assassin vipers,
Stabbing, biting. Painstaking was
The carnage, the ruddy morass—
The bleeding where wounds were imposed.
Each fatal gash quick birthed a ghost.

Such tales sermonized The Captain—
Anecdotal (like *Salvation*,
The derring-do of saints), voicing
Through tobacco, his rejoicing:
His pipe smoked out dodges of *Death*—
The preservation of his breath—
Thanks to providential *Mercy*.
(Blessings? Benefit of clergy!)

* Mispronounced (Anglo-style) as "Wipers."

Now, dear Papa couldn't foresee
1939—Germany
Assaulting Poland, September
1st, as if none could remember
World War 1's weaponized woes. (But
How else sell weapons—and profit?)

Those haunted years flaunted *Warning*:
"Brown Shirts" goose-stepping each morning
In Berlin, the buffoon blah-blah-
Blah of Hitler, his brouhaha
On radio or in the *Reichstag*—
His mug mucking up every mag—
His vicious strut, his mutt Fascists....

(But Adolf forgot: *Song* smashes
The concentration camp. Gershwin
Melodies fast besieged Berlin
Before either The Red Army
Or The Allies. Nazis, wary
Of *Jazz*, were correct—like Plato:
Music erects new concepts. So,
Even as cries bubbled up from
The rubble of The Blitz—mass bomb
Damage, and Stalingrad got starved—
Hitler flopped moot, mute, then larva'd
With embers, sparks, and squirming flame—
Cos his *Creed* did sundry defame,
Shot—gassed—in multiple Warsaws.
A bullet slammed, blew through his jaws,
And out his skull—like a mine blast:
He was ash—and we free at last
To draft a humane world where all
Could breathe equitably, equal.

I know this passage comes before
The start and end of sequenced war
[The Second]. But my clock circles
Back and forth. *History*'s circus
Mounts simultaneous acts, repeat
Shows: Lions that find their "tamers" sweet;
Fortune-tellers who guess deeds wrong;
Sorcerers hanged, oracles hung;
Trapeze artists who lose their grip;
Scared elephants that scared mice trip....
So, I canvass pasts and traverse
The *Future*—as swift as rhymed verse—
And discount timepieces and tomes,
Overshadowed by catacombs.)

Papa fathered churchgoers, but
I a child had—in wedlock out,
Displeasing the Captain. I was
Only 23, a novice
In life, not prepared to mother
My son. I granted another
Couple, childless, my blameless child
To love. I wasn't "loose" or "wild,"
But wished to be free, singular,
Alone, to thrive as a singer,
To ascend (with that liberty
And power a pilot feels) sky-high.

Papa did ask, "Portia, sing loud;
Lofty, make all us Negroes proud!"
To keep that commandment, my child
I could not keep. I curtsied, smiled
At audiences. Was that a sin?
To nurse *Lyric*, be nymph—in kin—
To Aeolus—to *Music*, pure?
Such was present-tense and future!

But to live by singing, how could
I succeed? I strove, as one should,
But choo-choo'd down to Dalhousie U.
To train to teach. Then, what? To pew
Classrooms, all black, was the sole choice:
I was "Miss White" with silver voice,
And "awful nice" as one pupil
Declared. But my pay was futile.

Never could I have afforded
The music schooling accorded
Europe's best. 20¢ an hour
Was my "worth," though *my* teacher—sour
Bertha Cruikshanks—charged $3.50
Per hour at the city's nifty
Conservatory of Music. But
I drank in those lessons! I caught
A train—or trudged—after teaching:
How else to reach stars worth reaching?
(First, you dream; next, you work to see
The dream edge to *Reality*.)

I directed the Cornwallis
Street Baptist Church choir; my solace
Was always *Song*. Our family
Staged musicals—for *Charity*—
During the Depression. Papa
Declaimed a 5-Year-Plan schema
(Pseudo-Socialist) to train blacks
For jobs beyond riding train tracks—
Or cooking or cleaning. Just as
Nazi Panzers were audacious
To mock the smoking braces
Of the Maginot Line, my basis
For local fame came from my wins—
2 years plus—of Haligonians'

Helen Campbell Kennedy Cup—
Silver (from which Champagne I'd sup
And sip) marking my triumphs twixt
1935 (fine year nixed
By Ethiopia's invasion by
Italy) and '38. I
Took the cup thrice; thus, it became
My own. Just one year lacked my name—
'36—because Captain White
Showed ill. Mortal as all are (quite);
Now, his haunt was his hospital
Bed. Dark dawn of his funeral,
Mourners blackened Halifax streets:
Hundreds counted thousands. Bright sheets
Of *Music* could not halt my blues.

Rev'rend—Captain—Dr.—we lose:
William Andrew White, a Doctor
Of Divinity. No doctor
Could save him though he could save souls.
His ring—now mine—I'm sure symbols
Good fortune: A Kraut-aimed bullet
Nicked it in The Great War. Gullet
My tears? I had to! He'd wanted
My world-success. I felt haunted
To achieve that. A granddaughter
Of slaves, born to a backwater,
If I could rise in Canada—
Garner note in America—
Reverse the Underground Railroad—
Win hearts and minds where slaves got sold—
Soar as songstress, wow each nation—
Obliterate "*Liberation*,"
The need for it, because to blot
Out *Discrimination*'s the plot;
Obliteration is also
Liberation; *Destruction*, though
Drastic, clears space, afresh, to dream.
(Think of Europe: The Marshall scheme—

To resurrect blasted cities,
Revive nations.... Fake pieties
Bear false witness.) But how could I
Proceed? My trifling salary—
A pittance! My future waxed dull....

Halifax Ladies Musical
Club backers heard me, then arranged
To fund all fees. No more estranged
I'd be from tutelage. Each lung
Would become an oasis of *Song*.
I'd pass from two-room school into
Auditoria of twice two
Hundred—because thousands of troops
In port, to board steamers and sloops
To World War Two battles, needed
Skits, tunes, and cheer. I succeeded
In leading acts; I'd jest and jump
And joke—and pratfall on my rump,
Masque in costumes and clown a part,
Or star, headline, croon out my heart
So hard, the accompanying
Piano wept as if living.

(To give all to *Art* is *Charity*
Or *Bankruptcy*? What parity
Exists betwixt artist and *Art*,
If not plastic wholeness of heart?
The artist is the ultimate
Penitent and novitiate,
Seeking to divine a vision,
Through *Art*, defy indecision,
And, to be perfect, be alert—
With chiaroscuro overt—
Without defect—perfect the work,
All firsts, all new, born out the Kirk
Of *Imagination*. Hardly
Could I descant songs dastardly....)

Enter Doc Ernesto Vinci—
Ph.D. in *Music, aussi*
M.D.—of course—in *Medicine*:
Jewish-dapper and Italian,
Too proud to bow to Benito—
Duce—Mussolini, to go
To North American exile
Was his score. Landing at the isle
Of Manhattan, he came on soon
To Halifax, to key each tune
With classical erudition.
Ghettoized, banned from *Medicine*,
He'd prescribe through *Music*. Well-known
In Italy for baritone
Lowings, he'd optimized operas
At La Scala…. He deemed my jazz
"Slinging" in department stores as
"Betraying *Talent*." His genius?
To prompt me to vaunt, flaunt, the show-
Stopping effects of *bel canto*
At the Conservatory of
Music. "Beautiful song," I love!
Such cooing suits my contralto.
No longer mezzo-soprano,
I purred folk songs in French, Spanish,
Then canted spirituals (English—
But "Negroid"), and epics German,
Then doctored breath, bettered diction.

Under "Da" Vinci's tutoring,
I joined words and notes, suturing,
And *Fame* was mine—only local
At first, but vast fans proved vocal,
And soon came the comparison
To *The* Marian Anderson,
That Negro American star
Of Europe's songs. Because—afar,

I seemed Canada's version, or
So some mused. But my voice could roar
Independent of simile
Or stereotype. I was *me*—
Not a copy, or second-class,
Nor second-fiddle. *Me* I was—
No echo of the States' "Black Swan,"
Nor shade! I was my own woman,
And showed regal stance, at 5-foot,
8 inches, with stage skills to boot:
I could dance, act, wisecrack, and sing.
Vinci made me try everything!
He'd even poke me neath the ribs—
To make me weigh my breath—its dribs
And gusts. I trilled—he judged—"Feelings";
That my manner wrought congealings
Of *Song* into *Poetry*. But, still,
Study is what transforms "I will"
Into "I did." *Accomplishment*
Isn't eked-out wish-fulfillment:
First comes *Work*, and, secondly, *Luck*:
Songs are sculptures, alive, unstuck.

To serenade soldiers, I felt
I shouldn't only bleat or belt
Broadway, movie anthems, or Pop
Smash hits, but also opera's top
Singles. Troops did stomp boots, and clap
Lustily. Bouquets capped my lap.
Others added a posh gesture:
Dear "boys" gifted me a silver
Pin. I was stupendously touched:
Applause verified *Love* they vouched.
Immeasurable—my pleasure
At their *Delight*! I *could* measure
Up to the concert stage, it seemed.
Reviewers wrote as I'd once dreamed—
Enchanted by my pluck and poise—
My "bell-like clarity of voice";

How "rich and pure" were all my notes.
I won valentines; I won votes!
And critics predicted that "Soon,
The globe, to Halifax, will tune…."

(*Song* was my *Art*—and job, but I—
A Negro citizen'd decry,
Privately, all damned *Injustice*.
I refute the lie that artists
Empty their art of politics!
Brothers Jack and Bill—no comics—
Kibbutzed with "Reds"—and deemed *Labour*
Rights salvation for each neighbour
In our commonweal. Paul Robeson
Prayed to Lenin, knelt to Stalin,
Gospelled "The *New* Soviet Union."
No, I'd not heed such "communion,"
But nor was I ever unsure
About where my heart leapt: Posture?
The "Left." Never was I unsure!
To every venomous gesture
Of *Fascisti*, I shouted back—
Plus gainst each white hating each black.
No figurehead, no figurine,
I sang against the serpentine,
Vampiric, moneybag-toting
Gangsters—Capitalists—voting
Against the *People* by branding
Public Spending as expanding
Government to uplift those down
And out, who crowd each shantytown.

And now I sing of Africville—
Never a slum—I don't cavil—
But a Coloured quarter that gives
No quarter where a Klansman lives.
Down here's where Duke Ellington'd come,
With his love, Mildred, to swill rum,
And court his "in-laws," The Dixons,
Whose piano fretted like vixens
In heat—squirming, squalling. But he'd
Task ivory and ebony—keyed
As one—breed finger-popping *Jazz*
Out of keyboard *Discord*. I was
Awful tempted to shake off coat
And forsake shoes, and shimmy bout
The Dixons' living room, while Duke
Plinked and plunked. No need for a juke
Box! All Africville was agog
To hear—squeak and squeal like a hog—
The Dixons' linoleum'd floors, as
Shoes, socks, bared feet—dizzied by *Jazz*—
Zigged and zagged and didn't dither
To zag and zig—hither, thither—
While Duke's digits slithered the keys.
I'd've loved've* scaled harmonies
Beside that maestro, to've** stepped
From my role as schoolmarm, and leapt
Up beside that piano—never
More alive, throbbing with fever—
Even though Duke's music would've
Upset Cap White…. Well, I *should've*!)

* "I would have loved to have": Contracted to—and pronounced as—
  four syllables.
** "To have": Contracted, yes, but still pronounced as two syllables.

IV – At War (1940–1945)

That I'd "bring Nova Scotia praise,"
This was said in the *War*-dark days
Of May, 1940, when Save
The Children Fund suffered a grave,
Income crisis. Slated to sing,
Shirley Blois took sick, cancelling
The child-welfare Benefit Show.
So I performed. My contralto
Delivery of spirituals
Blazed me a starlet. The burials
Of hurts in honeyed versicle—
The mix of gravel and treacle—
My patent style—growling, trilling—
Proved theatrical—and thrilling.

And so I became the darling
Of Halifax—her mint starling,
Prima donna. My only need?
A champion! Miss Edith Read—
Doctorated, a principal
Of Toronto's swank Branksome Hall
(Whose *filles* become leaders), sedate,
Designated my debut date—
7th of November '41—
At Auditorium Eaton—
To showcase me as "subversive"—
I.e. "sublime"—Proof-positive
Of ebon *Excellence*; to prove
Myself beyond New Scotland's love—
That I was a high star, shining
Above Atlantic saltwater-wave whining,
And so able to light the globe.
Incandescent was I! *The Globe
And Mail* critic didn't type bumf:
He hailed my "authentic triumph"!
I'd arrived! Well, at Toronto—
A chanteuse, belle at *bel canto*....

And so University Press
Of Oxford—managing my *Success*—
Mandated that I'd best now choose:
Seize headlines; reverse the recluse.
I quit school. My resignation
Wired up Africville. But, ration
My time, I had to! Africville
I ditched: Harlem boasts Sugar Hill!

Comport, transport, was I, to Manhattan!
Thanks to Miss Read, Edward Johnson—
The Metropolitan Opera
Manager—mandated Portia—
I—should debut at the Town Hall.
But first I trekked from Montreal
To Victoria, cross-Canada
(Quebec to Brit Columbia);
And my concert songbooks programmed
Spirituals because cannons blammed.
My tunes numbered arias because
Love's the *Good* that *Tragedy* flaws.
(Or so lovers dread.) In Saint John,
A soldier swooned, nose-dived down on
The floor, and a congregation
Wept, when I crooned the oration,
"Were You There." O! The power I felt
When I spied hankies pull from svelte
Purses and pockets to tamp eyes:
Surely I'd morphed from local prize;
Had bested all salt-spray hokum.
Now, no longer a gal at home
In overalls, I peered through haze
Haloing—that beautiful glaze
Of spotlights, floodlights. To New York
Destined, diverged I at that fork:
To vaunt dauntless *Art*; show Town Hall
My *Magnificence*; to enthrall!
My dressing-room flaunted a vase
Of flowers Halifax sent because

I should never ever forget
I was the East Coast's boast and bet—
Like the schooner coasting the dime—
The *Bluenose* (that *Pride* maritime).

Well, I did not. I ranged the stage
In calm command of *Song*'s language:
March 13, 1944—
With Doc Vinci—a thousand more—
Stretching to hear, from red plush seats
(Velvet), how I'd proclaim defeats
Of despots and each enslaver—
Nazi, Klansman; pitch palaver
Of "*Kalaignar*" (Tamil: Artist)
Gainst untoward—backward—fascist....

(While Uncle Sam's and Canada's
Flags ballyhoo'd our Allied cause,
I knew I sang beyond Town Hall—
I strove to smash every "Great Wall"
Separating us, each human
Being—similarly uncommon.)

To be a White was to uplift
"The Negro," no matter if, miffed
Were those who swore us "apes." I had
To descant angelic: "Not bad"
Was not good enough to answer
Every critic who thought "dancer"
The craft a "Negress," born, enacts.
(But *Intellect*, gymnastics acts:
Gravity-defying, each vault
Of thought mirrors a somersault.)
I was all "ye Olde South" disdained.
When I halted, thoroughly drained,
I was an empty vessel quite.
So, how did I conquer that night?
Ovations thrice. *The New York Times*
Enthused, "One of Heaven's own chimes"

Was I. The audience, overawed,
Saw "an angel" and heard "a god."
Columbia Concerts signed me
To a contract. Who would find me
Now had to look absurdly high,
Where the sun wanes, weak, shadow-nigh,
Dimmed by greater, more lustrous stars—
So all its luminescence chars....

But Nova Scotian and city
Governments, naming me, "pretty
Well ambassadorial," schemed
Up "The Portia White Fund." They dreamed
To prosper from my fame. Why not?
The war would end; we'd be—forgot—
We "Nova Scots." Two Assemblies
Judged it "savvy," not "niceties,"
To cash-back my cadences. Come
May 1944, to drum-
And-fife, I became a symbol
Of "New Scottish" style and appeal—
I mean, as much a draw, of sorts—
As that racing vessel (its ports
Now aborted, since it's long sunk),
Impressing dimes. (It's now a hunk
Of change.) My *State* gift? A white fox
Cape to grace concerts. Orthodox
Was I, the toast of Halifax
Et Nouvelle-Écosse. Them's the facts—
Of newsprint, iconoclastic
Idiosyncrasy. Plastic
Was I: Icon! Copacetic
As bleached-blonde, Vegas-synthetic,
Glitzed-up dolls (B-flick metaphor)—
Fifth Avenue fashion-plate or
Some "Slackers" (slang for Halifax)
Arriviste, gauche in tartan slacks—
Or *parvenue,* "Come-From-Away."
Yet, I love heels, pleat skirts that sway;

Highfalutin hats, mink as coat—
Some plaid, silk scarf kissing my throat....
Necessary accessory?
A purse (Mint-like—printing money)!
O! To window shop! In New York!
To down pound cake, "bubbly" uncork!
To knife sirloin or fork salmon,
Spoon spaghetti with chopped almon'!
And import and impart *Art Song*
And stage sage *Music*, now among
Suave Yanks (avid's their gravitas).

As the *War* got purged, upsurged *Jazz—*
Bebop—the clash of atoms primed
To jitterbug until each rhymed
In splitting, emitting a blast
So keen, ballads splintered—harassed
Until cacophonous, spastic.
(Hear chords—atonal, elastic.)

Journeyed I to Harlem at last
In 1944—August—
For the U.S. Negro Music
Festival. I was ecstatic
To hobnob with Langston Hughes, Fats
Waller, Tommy Dorsey—"cool cats"—
And Langston signed *The Dream Keepers*,
His poems, for me. I took sleepers
And coaches, tramped about the States;
Also, steamed to Scotia. The dates
Back home saw me rehearse right loud;
Halifax whelped a welcome crowd.
So I shook up Belle Aire Terrace
With my big voice. So much *Solace*
Was there among the "Bluenoses"—
Those homeys who tossed me roses,
And whose slang plumbed dumb *Prejudice*;
But could also be so darn nice.

Once, down home, I vroomed to Canning,
To find Mr. Eaton, planning
To nurse a "Portia apple." I
Sent sis sloshing in plush rain. Why
Soaked she was, but presto'd Eaton!
Then's "Portia" supported eatin!
When I sang earnest approval,
Ernest Eaton's blush was novel:
He took the tint of "my" apple!

When home, enchanting each chapel,
Spooning up spirituals extra sweet—
So saints swooned at Cornwallis Street
Baptist Church, I urged my brother,
Lorne, to snatch degrees. Another
Relative perused *Law*; later,
I heard he said, "no one greater"
Than I did Don Oliver meet.
(So kind a mensch, his kind's elite.)

The *War* daggered on; I appeared
Again at Town Hall, now sponsored
By the National Council of
Negro Women. They showed such *Love*—
For I amplified us: Negro;
Stately, as well, in Toronto,
When crooning for Allied *victoire*,
And in N.S., basked I in *gloire*—
The scores of standing ovations!
But on Halifax vacations,
It wasn't kosher to visit
Hotel restaurants: I'd "upset
The other guests"—white clientele....
Once, the desk clerk at one hotel
Told me I wasn't "suitable"
To dine with others. Decibel-
Level high, I countered: "How will
You explain the charge on my bill
For Room Service? The Government
Of Canada funds my talent,

Is bankrolling my stay. They'll find
It weird that in my room I dined;
That I had a private waiter.
Do tell?" To the elevator,
The rust-flushed clerk led me, and I
Descended to dine—most finely.

But so alone I always was—
Denied diva leads in operas:
Almost always a solo black,
And never a contralto, crack
Enough for a marquee-lit part,
Though I knew star roles whole—by heart.
The cause of these faults? *Racism*!
Progress paralyzed! (*Fascism*
Is preferable because it's
Bad-ass plain—a bare-knuckle *Blitz*.
The fascist drags a razor cross
Eyes; or grabs blades and stabs.) "Their loss,"
I laugh, but *Pain* throbs within. Tours
Of the U.S. exposed cruel mores—
The Ku Klux Klan disguised as cops—
Negroes gunned down in traffic stops....
Always did Canada I like—
Opposing the Dixie "Third Reich"—
Its clandestine Hitlers, Tojos,
Their *War*-like crimes versus Negroes—
As if its Constitution'd been
Scrawled by muggers and by madmen—
As democratic as garbage.
(Outrages boomerang from *Rage*—
As hurled slurs ping-pong off police,
The Supreme Court's primal *Malice*.)

There we were, all battling Nazis,
But homespun monsters and harpies
Rampaged, spewing fulsome *Hatred*.
I lobbed em notes bowel-created

Cos bigots merit *Spite*. I showed
Vinci's spiky temperament. Owed
A hearing, always, I'd intrude—
Beatitudes of Negritude:
Blackness! My permanent costume—
Lucence that lectrifies Goth gloom.

Because I'm a public symbol
Of dreams that all folks be equal,
I don't hobnob with limousine
Types, whose visages glaze each screen,
Their cigarettes, cigars, idling,
While their shoulders and chins, cradling
Phones, ape labourers, play at *Work*;
But all are shams. Easy to shirk,
They are. The *hoi polloi*, I choose—
Who warble hymns and wail the *Blues*—
Honest in their hearts, not blasé:
My best fans. Let paparazzi
Hammer my face flat as headlines—
Celebrity of their designs—
The songstress gussied up in gowns,
Hustled on stage, grinning through frowns—
Rustling up songs, my corpuscles
Queueing to cue the spirituals—
Soulful, heart-wrenching moans and groans:
Not gutless sighs, nor feeble drones.

Yet, I don't forget why I star—
To model *Excellence*, disbar
Stereotypes swearing "Negro
Inferiority." To show
Us as iron, steel, or gold-plated.
I am th'unanticipated
Advocate, arriving, breathing
Adrenalin, angry, seething,
Striving to *Truth* tell the utmost
(*Sincerity* fosters *glasnost*,
Part by part); to capitalize
On facts and decapitate lies;

To hurl out—with noble spittle—
Bit by bit, little by little,
The Autobio of *The Race*—
To always exceed ceded place.

But that doesn't mean I'm some drab—
"All work, no play": A scraped-up scab!

Thus, "V.E. Day"—when *Victory
In Europe* was won, people's *Glee*
Made em thirsty, but Government
Locked-down liquor: "No argument!"
Well, soldiers and sailors, happy
To have outlived *War*, and scrappy
For a mug or tumbler or jig,
Ran wild! Only the prude or prig
Would tolerate forced *Temperance*
On such a "holiday"! This chance
To celebrate *Triumph* required
Liquor—as servicemen desired....
So, stores got looted and trolleys
Set ablaze. Glass broke in volleys
As bottles drained or windows bust:
The *Riot* expressed civic *Lust*
For unrepressed *Joy* in living
When so many'd died. Forgiving
Of the *Mayhem* was I, for I
Was thirsting too! I did rely
On a pal to sneak—slip—into
A sacked shop and bring back some brew.
He lugged us home a box, clinking
Nicely, venting chinks like drinking
Vessels (bottles, I imagined).
But as quick as the box opened,
Vanished was the thought that vanquished
Foes could be roasted: O! Banished
Was that hope! We peered into the
Box: No booze, just shards of china....

v – Victory and Sorrow (1946–1955)

*N*ot the interrupted memoirs
Of neckline amputees*, our choirs
Warn of police peeping through holes—
Lurking like wolves, slinking like moles—
Snooping through closets, down chimneys....
We cry of nights of deportees
Yo-yoing back as fugitives
Or buckled in shocking chairs. Lives
On? *Slavery*? Yes, of a sort—
Negro chain-gangs okayed by court:
Judges forcing Negroes to slave
For jailhouse businesses, and have
No future but a litany
Of lashes, the monotony
Of *Evil*. Thus, our spirituals
Spoil all routine memorials; To be historical is, for
Us, to go hysterical. Sure,
Our story's glorious. But when
Can we—as citizens—begin
To live freely, live as we want,
And not face white-hoods—ghastly, gaunt—
Who haunt us with vile histories?

Tarzan—in top hat—spreads *Disease*—
The cancerous idea that
"Chalk" must rule folks of Colour. [What
Animated *Apartheid* was
That credo in South Africa's
Laws.]** Cast out mints and coffeecake:
Nought repairs our split-stone heartbreak—
Cleavages through which rivulets
Torrent and tumble in wild jets—
In poetics—chaotic, savage,
Decrying *Savagery* average

* Cf. The Nuremberg Trials.
** Editorial interjection.

To empires raised on *Racism*—
Inhumane as *Terrorism*—
As consequential as critics
(*Incivility* as *Civics*)—
Ambitious amateurs starved for
Applause—judges who back *de jure*
Segregation, their white gloves clean—
Their Al Jolson blackface serene....
"*Harmony* cannot be enforced,"
They say. But God's our source (divorced
From petty human *Grievance*) of
Freedom and that smoky salve, *Love*.

Our station in *Life* (or *Strife*) is
Our baggage, luggage—*History*'s
Garbage—the burden we endure.
Why else value too scarce *Rapture*?
The promise each spiritual whispers
In churches immured in murmurs
As indignant as dawn sunlight—
Ungraspable allure of *Right*—
Righteousness, Justice. No sooky
Babies, we deem special—spooky—
The tenured lyrics that recall
Slavery, the Civil War, all
Dogmatically hemophiliac—
Bleeding hotly each whip-lashed back—
Or cracking like a flawed prism—
Or mirrors smashed by *Fascism*,
Now bundled in their shattering;
Resembling fire—a smattering.
The Axis Pact are now vassals
Of us Allies—all their castles
Splay in ruins under our missiles.
Europe, which forged blacks' manacles,
Now's a *Blues*-trumpet swamp, paleface-
Dotted, in indigo night-space.

Spy the squalid dazzle of Stars
And Stripes—the U.S. flag: Victors
As democrats? One takes as joke
These red-blood, white, blue-ribbon folk—
Supposedly A-1, O.K.
Christians, holy as a sun-ray....
Yet, down Dixie, each hypocrite
Plays Grand Ole Opry, Ku Klux twit—
As wicked as the nails in Christ's
Ankles and palms. Cold *Artifice*:
That's their eyes, their hearts. *Machismo*—
Theirs—is a *Genocide* gizmo,
But what they're most profligate at
Is paying out pennies, so that
Wages sign workers' concessions.

(Press down the poor with "Depressions"!
That's their mobster-like common sense.
Their hypocritical "innocence"
Pretends to *Charity*, and they
Act slick, swish about, just sashay,
As if their stealing weren't the cause
Of foreclosures that breed outlaws.
And none of their sins is final....)

Th'enveloping sound of vinyl
Would capture the vaporous voice—
Issued *ex* my high-class bodice—
Proclaim this dame a royal woman;
I.D. my Song of Solomon
Lips (plum-like comely), my ebon,
North Atlantic eyes uncommon....

I produce no snippets of lays—
Concoct no cut-short, choked-back phrase—
Instead belt the heart-felt stanza,
Verse on verse. Extravaganza
Is my standard. As in Quito,
Ecuador, above mosquito

And vaulting clouds, I was the first
To line-out songs where lungs can burst—
At 10,000 feet, mid Andes
Peaks. Peasants handed me candies,
Then a silver bowl. Next event?
Tour Panama! My gold present?
A gilt medal from the Isthmus
Negro Youth Congress. Glamorous
In my sonorous descanting,
I left no audience "wanting":
Each is as voracious as poets'
Mouths are for words. I played to wits,
And critics had to plagiarize
Thesauruses to fit their sighs
To synonyms, to uniquely
Laud my lungs. No quip obliquely
Read, but gave palpable surmise,
Heralding honeyed enterprise—
Even lustful and gluttonous
New York, natural mutinous—
Impossible to satisfy—
Addressed me plaudits, praise, sky-high:
As vivacious as perfume, swelled
The acclaim. My name got misspelled
As "Porsche"—like the pricey car.
My "resonant, God's avatar
Voice," now craved a *brio* photo—
Publicity (autobio)....

Via his eye—Armenian—
(Silversmith-like, Smithsonian)—
Yousuf Karsh organized to snap
My image for his stellar map—
A galaxy of luminous
"Mug-shots"—Winston Churchill (minus
Cigar), greyed Hemingway, Georgia
O'Keeffe. Not shy, I was PORTIA—
And sparkled, haloed, kindled by
A spotlight—a sable *houri*—

A black angel encircled by
Angular shimmer. God knows why!
Oft snapped, but too poor to afford
Karsh's exposure—a record
Cover (perhaps) or photo stills,
I wooed his *Charity*. The spills
Of developer ignited:
My image came—black, back-lighted—
Emphasis embroidered my eyes.
"Belle!" Exclaimed the artist. My prize?
Crisp, complimentary radiance—
Black-and-white, light-suffused "Romance"—
So rich chiaroscuro reigns.
Karsh declared he took "untold pains"
To highlight my *Sincerity*—
"Persuasive *Personality*"....
(I knew he'd snapped Art Rubenstein,
Menuhin *sans* his violin,
Landowska *sans* her harpsichord,
But Horowitz with his keyboard,
And did highlight their *Scintillance*.
How I prayed for such surveillance!)
My negatives? So positive!
Black *Beauty* framed superlative.
(Undiminished *Celebrity*
Accords deathless *Vivacity*?)

Fire is a tissue of sun, and
Apparent in scorched, torching sand,
And in torrid heat Saharan
And candid in the Caribbean—
Where I was, once—3 months—the star—
"Black-haired *bellezza*," "scimitar
Of *Beauty*," "Sensuous, solo
Siren," "the Divine Contralto"....
The epithets—epicurean
In *Taste*—were like lightning-swollen
Clouds or scaffolding of sunbeams,
Their unfolding in golden reams,

All framing my being, this branding
Popular on every landing:
In Curaçao and Grenada,
In Bogotá (Colombia),
In Barbados and Jamaica,
Ecuador and Panamá,
Where I received a special book
Of spirituals (those songs that spook).
My odyssey was beautiful,
Hectic; my brain o'er-brimmed my skull.
Appropriate was the epic
Journey, but *Fate* tracks the tragic....

Between Nova Scotia, New York,
Every path—played out—splayed a fork.
Elegies freeze *Decay*, I trust—
But still my steel got brushed with rust.
My Columbia Records team
Could not plot how to chart my dream:
To throw concerts? Cut a record?
Bray *R & B*?*—a Pop blackbird?
To be "Negro" or "just" a *chanteuse*?
To stick to type or just bust loose?
Be *avant-garde* or slave to trends?
Agents drove me to my wits' ends.
Nor did I know how to break free
Of buttoned-down clerks, deaf to me.
If words were had, I had no say.
Concerts fell short; fell short my pay.

Then, *Health*, that *Wealth* (*Truth* all patients
Know), went bust—with complications.
Too much strain expropriated—
The gains misappropriated—
My vocal cords. Five years a queen—
'41 to '46: *Spleen*

* Rhythm and Blues.

Spieled damned *Judgment*: I'd have to pause!
I was no longer what I was
On stage. "Star turns" since '41....
Now my throat throbbed. Its tone? Gone!

Truth: *Cancer* cancels *Song*! Syrups
Couldn't salve corroded chirrups.
(*Cancer* is as pejorative
As wounds, and just as normative.)
I was a Lapsang Souchong leaf,
Gusted by smoky *Song—Belief*
In wild hopes. But good *Luck* turned flirt—
As sparse as dew in a desert.

I'd winged so high, mere *Gravity*
Looked a myth. The grave's cavity
Remains too real, though. I sank low—
Like cinnamon o'ercome by snow.
No matter copious rose petals—
Silver bowls and golden medals—
I slunk in theatres of mortal
Pain and surgery. Now curtal,
A spinster, all alone....

                                            Murray
Bonnycastle chanced *Chivalry*:
My "Prince Charming," he inked me poems—
"Romantic," mimicking down home's
Glee club ballads. So devoted,
He even moaned blues, but quoted
Dante, crediting, "Lyric is
Love." Was that so? And was I his?
Was it possible? For *Travel*
Undoes couples; we unravel....
Travel spurs *Imagination*,
But it also harms. No nation
Proves a comfy home.... Aberrant
As shadows, I sobbed, *"Ubi sunt"*:

"Where is the love that'll let me rest—
Heroine upon a hero's chest?"
Hoisted me on a pedestal,
Aye, Murray did! I was diastole
To his systole, though. Our rhyming
Was offbeat. Our hearts weren't chiming
In tune. No, not enough to please
Me and summon ample release
From *Ambition.*

                              I still wanted
To stay *the* star. I was haunted
By being near-famous: The worst *Fame*!
Better unknown than have a name
Only some folks know. But worse than
Half-fame is *Infamy*—trashcan
Stashed with *Envy* plus *Sloth*—"last straws"
That once-friends dubbed the doubled flaws
Of each other. So, Ruth Wilson—
Mon ami, hostess at Moncton—
Alleged Miss Read my "exploiter"
Or a "permissive dictator,"
While Read ranted I was "stupid"—
And that Vinci is no Cupid,
Nor angelic, but cupidic—
I.e. greedy (not *impudic,**
Only guilty of *Avarice*
For profile, to see his "genius"
Broadcast), while Ernesto did mark
My "decline" as my doing. His bark
Snagged, nagged—jagged like a dog-bite.
He swore I lazed! An oversight—
Objectively—was that "allege"!
Once-friends now used canine language

* Romanian: Impudent, improper.

To bitch at all (Latin cusses
To which the damned are unconscious—
Though still hurtful as spat, prosaic
Slurs, Tijuana-Bibles comic).
Libel is silent, but *Slander*
Is loud. I wished to meander,
To mosey, or to mediate—
To end bluster and *Truth* orate:
My slide—my fall—was no friend's fault....

Jazz and *Rock-n-Roll* fixed assault
On *Tradition*'s bastions. Elvis
Presley and Chuck Berry—pelvis-
Twisters—were jitterbugging like
Electro-shocked monkeys. The "mic"—
Which I'd never liked—was attuned
Now to crooners and crank words crooned—
Those syllables enigmatic
As a phlegmatic priest. Vatic
Souls—each one—just failed to predict
That brash drum bashing could evict
Beethoven, Bach, and Brahms—amiss;
That bad grammar could score Grammys....

(Unpredictable folderol
Bamboozles now each concert hall,
And no fustian protestation
Alters this contralto's station....)

Hearing *Music*, I was never
A snob, but *Rock-n-Roll*'s ever
Antithetical to *Music*—
At least that eggheads term, "*Classic*."
But *Rock* makes its fans feel alive—
To jump, jitterbug, and jive—
And seems authentic to the heart—
E'en if it's hard to call it *Art*.

Then again, *Ragtime, Blues,* and *Jazz*
Seldom get classed as *Art* because
Negroes are never "geniuses"—
No matter that one's ingenious
In composition or in voice
Or in fingering or in choice
Of instrument, instrumental
To *Artistry* monumental.
So, I shan't be prejudiced now
Versus Top 40 radio—
That Pop mixture of *Rock-n-Roll*
And *Rhythm-n-Blues* (now dubbed *Soul*).

VI – Teacher / Singer Unto Eternity

*S*elected to teach. Singing
Belonged to a concert setting
To which I no longer belonged.
My "right" to stardom now felt wronged;
A "curtain recomposing" was
How I recast this shift. Because
My limelight-time was now long-lost,
No bitterness wracked me, to host
A whack of pupils in my home,
Planted in Toronto, to roam
The globe no more. My intention
Was not to annul the mention
Of "golden this and silver that"—
To melt down medals in a vat
And feel genteel *Degradation*—
Remorseful *Degeneration*—
And post, to the foreboding dump,
Eroded *Circumstance* and *Pomp*—
Enduring a circus—curses—
"*Self-Annihilation*" versus
A tsunami of parasites—
Critics' backbiting overbites....

El Trabajo—The Work—remained:
To transform novices I'd trained—
Strained—into dazzling, dauntless types—
Striking a star's stand, miking pipes!
Singing begins in the gut—and
Gets upheld by the spine. One must stand
Adroit and edgy, but able
To gesture, dance, cakewalk, stable
In stance—to yield the maximum
Iota of *Grace*, strike royals dumb,
So that excellencies bow, wowed
By insolent posture, unbowed.

(Think Dot Dandridge, her *Carmen Jones*:
Hands on hips, swivelling steeled bones,
Her attitude feisty—a bull's,
Knocking loose crowns off cringing skulls!)
My pupils learn *Song's Heritage*—
To elevate, through breath's carriage—
Mortals—to the portals God wrought.

I'm riven—divided by *Thought*
Or *Memory*—the diary of
Mortality. Where went my *Love*?
To God Who warrants it? Or *Song*?
To thrive a while—*alive*—among
Musical notes, song sheets, only
To leave a perfumed corpse? Lonely
I was, have been, and dying all
The same—as if I were a doll—
Eyes blinking, closing each "curtain"
Temporarily, uncertain,
Until that final curtain call....

All my enrolled received my "all":
On that gilt roster, find Lorne Greene,
Dinah Christie, Don Francks, and e'en
Robert Goulet—stellar students—
Stars on stage or screen.... *Prudence*
Suggests I refrain from toasting—
Or what could be dissed as boasting—
My clientele. Instead, I'll state
My teachers: Gina Cigna—late
Of Paris, France—and wise Irene
Jessner—two sopranos, serene—
Prima donnas of the world stage,
God's concoctions! Such tutelage
They awarded! *Mea culpa*
Was my refrain when *fa-so-la*
I got wrong. And the *coup de grâce*?*
My unseen blushing! *Ooh-la-la*!

* Pronounced "coo-de-gra."

From 1955, I, yes,
Commenced to die. Cancer's *Distress*
Throttled my *Song*-concert-giving,
Only God's *Strength* stirred my living.

(Incorruptible the *Future*
Is, for it never arrives pure;
Only as a version, undreamt—
Of the *Present*—always unkempt.)

In 1959, I clad
In patchwork rags, played brash and bad
Tituba, the sable "witch" of
Salem, Mass., who witnessed a trove
Of demons trouble teenage girls,
She testified. Soon, thanks to swirls
And curlicues of scriptured lies,
Innocents dropped from gallows' ties—
The noose. But Tituba survived.
I fleshed her figure, as revived
By Arthur Miller in his play
The Crucible, which is, I'll say,
A tragedy, satirizing
"Witch-hunts" for "Commies." Surprising
Was my taking a part that says,
"Conspiracies, hysterias,
And hypocrites, all imperil
Democracy"? No! So sterile
Of mind I'd be could I not think
For myself and stand—at the brink,
Even of *Opprobrium*—like
Robeson and Anderson, and strike
The set and stride the stage and speak
Out for *Justice*! (What else to seek?)

I saluted The Queen and Prince—
But then, lastly, I didn't wince
To lilt spirituals to Baptists—
Our World Federation. That was—is—
My last concert: July of
1967—"One Love"
For "The Summer of Love" that year.
For, "all one needs is *Love*," not *Fear*,
(This The Beatles pledge). The fissures
Of *Song*—the caesuras, fixtures
Of *Silence*, let us contemplate—
Our corps' inhale, exhale (innate)—
The troughs twixt each birth-and-death date—
How *Absence* must *Presence* truncate—
Next, the "Next World" awaiting us—
Invisible, or tenuous,
Where tumbled down, crumbled remains
Reinvigorate. *Soul* attains
Its sounding in volcanic *Song*—
Lightning-satiated, each lung
Volleys, smoking, each thundered note,
So that, "retaliatory"—quote,
Unquote—"as Pushkin," the song shows
Victorious fire. That's no pose!
Poesy ain't flimflam: It's flame!

The errant apprentice? My name:
I, me! I'm what *Memory* sings.
Handy are my extended wings:
Again I defy *Gravity*
Nimbly, arcing, with levity,
To that space of sonorous airs—
Where *Music*'s perfume, unawares,
And one sings notes that one inhales
Sweeter than can sound nightingales....
Flowers flute, wherever I roam:
Heaven hath become my home.

Biography of Portia May White

Born on June 24, 1911, in Truro, Nova Scotia, Portia May White was the third child of Izie Dora White and William Andrew White. Her father, a Virginian, had been born in 1874, only nine years after the extirpation of African Slavery in the United States, a fact which made Portia only the second generation to be born outside of legal bondage. Portia's Nova Scotian mother, Izie, had African-American, British, and Mi'kmaw heritage. Though Andrew (his preferred name) and Izie had a December-May marriage, exchanging vows when he was thirty-two and she just sixteen, theirs was a love-match, producing thirteen children, ten of whom survived to adulthood. Portia grew up with nine siblings, seven her juniors.

Importantly too, after having relocated to Nova Scotia in the 1890s, Andrew had become one of the first African-Nova Scotians (or Africadians) to earn a university degree, a Bachelor of Arts from Acadia University (which also awarded him an honorary doctorate in 1936), and he entered the ministry as a Baptist pastor. For her part, Izie sang soprano and played piano. These parental backgrounds ensured that Portia's childhood embraced multiculturalism, cosmopolitanism, humanity, and "The Humanities" (music and languages). Named for a feminist heroine from Billy Shakespeare's nasty comedy, *The Merchant of Venice* (1596–99), a penchant for theatre informed Portia's girlhood psyche. She dreamt that, one day, she'd parade across stages, bow before audiences, and bask in rapturous ovations.

Certainly, as a schoolgirl, Portia's talent demarcated her as special, but she also starred in the choir at her father's church. His sermons were riveting and elegant, but Portia's voice added the enchanting and thrilling touches of song. Portia began her church choir singing once aged eight, and, still that young, she entered a music contest with a sister, singing as sopranos over radio. Indeed, just as Reverend William Andrew White was pioneering the use of radio to broadcast his suave voice and professorial preaching around the Maritimes and down to the "Boston States," so did he also allow his children's voices, including Portia's, to astonish, inspire, and uplift his listeners.

Thanks to his Great War patriotic service as the first African-descended person to be named an officer in the British Army, so that he could assist in directing the segregated No. 2 Construction Battalion in the south of France (1916–18), Andrew became an African-Canadian figure of national and international stature. His prestige unlocked doors for Portia that her talent then blew wide open. Still, she needed professional training as a singer (never of blues tunes, which Andrew loathed) and she needed a job to help pay for the lessons.

At age eighteen, Portia began to teach—in a black-only school in Africville, Nova Scotia. But her income was too paltry to cover her musical education. To find more opportunities to sing—and to learn—she took over her father's church choir.

At age twenty-three, in 1934, just as she was starting her stage career, Portia had a son, but gave him to others to raise. Soon, due to her beautiful, mezzo-soprano solos, Portia thrice won the Helen Campbell Kennedy Cup, in 1935, 1937, and 1938. Her perpetual receipt of this silver trophy led to its being gifted to Portia.

When Andrew passed away in 1936, mourners filled his church and throngs lined Halifax's streets. He was a beloved leader, but died before he could witness Portia's triumphs, which coincided with the duration of World War II.

For one thing, the war (or rumours of war) brought Dr. Ernesto Vinci, a Jewish Italian M.D. and a classical, operatic baritone, to Halifax, where, not permitted to practice medicine (due to anti-Semitic restrictions), he taught music at the local Conservatory. Portia became his star pupil, mastering *bel canto*, while the Halifax Ladies' Musical Club took care of her tuition.

Simultaneously, new stages opened up for Portia, for thousands of troops required entertainment and inspiration as they milled about Halifax, waiting to ship out across the killing fields of the U-Boat–trolled Atlantic to march eventually onto the battlefields of Europe.

In high demand in Halifax, Portia sang jazz in department stores and operatic bits in amateur theatres, while transitioning to a contralto voice, *via* constant practice under Vinci's direction. Replacing another singer for a charity benefit, in 1940, Portia wowed Haligonian critics with her spirituals.

Nettie Evelyn Potts

June
1928

Evelyn Potts 1928

Mother

Nettie

Billie Father

Mildred

George June Helena

Portia
1929

Portia, Bernice Earle
Blanche Adams and Susie Parker
June, 1929

Also loving Portia's voice was Dr. Edith Read, who arranged for her a November 7, 1941, concert at Toronto's Eaton Auditorium. Another triumph! Thus, Portia left her Africville school post, undertook tours North-East-West-South to practically every town and nook, every city and cranny, of Canada.

Despite a brief time-out for throat surgery in 1943, Portia was ready for her Manhattan debut on March 13, 1944. *The New York Times* and other critics had to scour their thesauruses to find the right superlatives to describe the voice they'd heard. World fame seemed certain for Portia....

Now, Portia garnered the financial support of the City of Halifax and the Province of Nova Scotia, who realized that, just as the schooner *Bluenose* and Longfellow's epic *Evangeline* had captivated American imaginations, helping to usher tourists to our harbours and shores, so could Portia's fame perhaps also stoke American interest in "New Scotland." The two governments created The Portia White Fund—now known as the Nova Scotia Talent Trust—to assist her quest for sustained, international, concert-stage stardom.

After other acclaimed shows in New York and Toronto, Portia was welcomed to Panamá, Colombia, Curaçao, Barbados, Jamaica, Grenada, and Ecuador, spending one-fourth of 1946 in the Caribbean and Central and South America. In Panamá, a youth group presented her with a gold medal.

Sadly, the "Latin" sojourn turned out to be the height—and the end—of Portia's major, public concerts. Diagnosed with cancer, she became the subject of scalpels, not microphones. She decided to settle in Toronto to be closer to doctors and surgeons privy to her illness and attentive in their treatments.

Contributing to the cessation of Portia's touring career too were the disputes among her friends—Vinci and Read and Ruth Wilson. Moreover, her New York agents couldn't figure out how to market her. Although she was managed by Columbia Records, amazingly, no one there thought to ask her to cut a record. Her fame as a concert singer came by word-of-mouth due to first-person witnessing. She was a world-class singer who never became a recording artist, and, so, lost the opportunity to become a star in mono or stereo or on LPs or even on 45s.

Retiring from the stage completely in 1952, she became a voice and music teacher, based—first—at Branksome Hall, the Toronto fiefdom of her supporter, Dr. Read. Later, Portia offered studies in music and song in studios that she established in the various Toronto apartments in which she lived. Portia's fame attracted star pupils: Lorne Greene, Don Francks, Dinah Christie, Judy Lander, and Anne Marie Moss.

In 1959, Portia took the role of Tituba in a Canadian television production of Arthur Miller's anti-intolerance play, *The Crucible*. It is likely that she played other roles in otherwise unsung, unheralded, and unremembered stage and/or radio shows.

In 1964, Portia enjoyed one last hurrah: A Command Performance before Her Majesty Queen Elizabeth II at the brand-new Confederation Centre in Charlottetown, Prince Edward Island. On February 13, 1968, Portia vanished from the world, but is now to be found among the stars.

It was only after her death that an album appeared, consisting of tracks culled from tapes of live performances. Soon, other memorials and commemorations began to materialize. The Nova Scotia Talent Trust began to bestow The Portia White Award upon superior vocalists; the Nova Scotia Government presents annually The Portia White Prize (since 1998) for exceptional artists from any discipline; Canada Post issued a postage stamp to honour Portia in 2000. That same year, Sylvia Hamilton released her documentary *Portia White: Think On Me*, which received national broadcast on Canadian Broadcasting Corporation, Bravo, and Vision television concerns. Citadel High School in Halifax now boasts the Portia White Atrium.

Although Portia never crossed the threshold from promise to sustained achievement, she remains the first African-Canadian (and African-Canadian woman) to become an international concert sensation. In this sense, Oscar Peterson (1925–2007), the stellar jazz pianist from Montreal, followed in her footsteps, as do—arguably— Measha Brueggergosman, Alessia Cara, Drake, The Weeknd—and, maybe, one day, you.

Acknowledgements

Background information for this poem is derived from Lian Goodall's bio, *Singing Towards the Future: The Story of Portia White* (Toronto: Napoleon Publishing, 2004). I also made useful visits to the public museum exhibit "Celebrating Portia White...50 years on," housed at Don Heights Unitarian Congregation, Toronto, Ontario, February 3–28, 2018, and curated by my cousin (and Portia's), namely, Sheila White. My student assistant in the summer of 2017, Ms. Celia Pang, also researched the story of Ms. White. Portia White's nephew—my cousin—the folksinger Chris White of Ottawa and another cousin, namely, the historian Nancy Oliver-Mackenzie of Montreal, extended me comments and advice that I've not always been wise enough to utilize. Still another cousin, the poet and filmmaker Sylvia Hamilton of Wolfville, reviewed this story to pinpoint incorrect info, extraneous commentary, and infelicitous (or erroneous) diction. I thank her, too, for her sage insights to which I have sometimes preferred the outré.

The poem was written in Toronto (ON); Richmond (BC); aboard Air Canada 182 (YVR-YYZ, Seat 18C); aboard Via Rail Canada Train 60 (Guildwood-Montreal, Car 3, Seat 13C); in Montréal (QC); aboard VIA Rail Canada Train 67 (Montreal-Oshawa, Car 4, Seat 5C); in Oshawa (ON); aboard GO Transit Train 933 (Oshawa-Guildwood); aboard Air Canada 103 (YYZ-YVR, Seat 12C); and in Nanaimo (BC); between 16 *mars* mmxviii & 4 *avril* mmxviii. Next, I edited it aboard GO Transit Train 906 (Guildwood-Oshawa); in Oshawa (ON); aboard VIA Rail Train 62 (Oshawa-Montréal, Car 3, Seat 13C); in Montréal (QC); aboard VIA Rail Train 63 (Montréal-Oshawa, Car 6, Seats 13C, then 14A); and aboard GO Transit Train 921 (Oshawa-Guildwood); and in Toronto (ON); between 30 *septembre* mmxviii & 5 *octobre* mmxviii. Further editing was undertaken in Halifax (NS), at The Lord Nelson Hotel, 5-7 *décembre* mmxviii. I made a final pass through the manuscript at the Air Canada Maple Leaf Lounge at Pearson (YYZ), then at Stanfield (YHZ), and aboard Air Canada 620 (YYZ-YHZ, Seat 18E) and Air Canada 7754 (YHZ-YYG, Seat 9B), all on 22 *août* mmxix. I furthered the editing in Room 229 of the Rodd

Charlottetown Hotel, 22–26 *août*, and at YYG on 26 *août*, and in Toronto (ON) on 26–28 *août* mmxix. It was re-edited, thrice, by Paul Zemokhol (as is my/our standard practice).

The fine artist Lara Martina, once a Nova Scotian and now (again) an Italian citizen, committed to illustrating this story years ago, when it was slated to be a children's book. I'm very pleased that the bio has moved into the YA category, allowing her to be as open in her *Art* as her Muse desires. I also smile at the Nova Scotian-Italian connection in her life that is mirrored in the mentor-protégé relationship between Ernesto Vinci and Portia White.

Along with the support of the E. J. Pratt Professorship, sustained by Dr. Sonia Labatt and Victoria University (at the University of Toronto), other organizations also contributed to my in-transit authorship: Kwantlen Polytechnic University—Surrey (BC), City of Nanaimo (BC), Dalhousie University—Halifax (NS), and the Prince Edward Island Writers' Guild—Charlottetown (PEI). At Nimbus, Whitney Moran was the unfailing champion of this book and also its direct catalyst.

My late father—Bill Clarke—and his mom, Nettie (Portia's sister and my grandmother), tutored my brothers and me, as boys, in the greatness of Portia. I remember many Sunday visits to Nanny Clarke's parlour, where, in hushed, reverential tones, we would turn the pages of a photo album that depicted Portia's shimmering career. So, for me, my great-aunt has always been the premier example of Africadian artistic achievement!

I thank those relatives who have served to preserve so splendidly Portia's legacy. As does, given her middle name, my beloved daughter and artist, Aurélia.

Portia White was, in every way, extraordinary. Rightly is her signature song, "Ride On, King Jesus," a spiritual that declares, "No man can a-hinder me!" Right on!

Lastly, I thank my darling, poet Giovanna Riccio, a pillar of *Conscience* and a pillow of *Kindness*. Always unhindered is her love; always triumphant is her thought.

Colophon

The text of *Portia White: A Portrait in Words* is set in Warnock Pro Light. Warnock Pro is a typeface designed by Robert Slimbach and first published in 2000. This font is a classic-looking, old style, serif typeface commissioned by Chris Warnock in honor of his father, John Warnock, the co-founder of Adobe Systems. John Warnock's visionary nature led to major advances in desktop publishing and graphic arts software.